A Year of Kindness

Pamela Paresky, PhD

Discover how journaling about
kindness leads to a happier,
more meaningful life.

For my wonderful family, my steadfast friends,
and my extraordinary teachers.

If I am not for myself, who will be for me?

But if I am only for myself, what am I?

If not now, when?

Rabbi Hillel (Ethics of the Fathers, 1:14)

Why journal about kindness and gratitude?

Happiness is elusive. Yet, for much of our lives we relentlessly pursue it. For some, the search for happiness becomes an obsessive quest for pleasure and self-gratification. Others are consumed with examining what happened in the past that inhibits their ability to be as happy as they would like to be. For still others, the pursuit of happiness develops into a preoccupation with wealth and success.

During the height of the stock market boom, social psychologists asked, "If we are so rich, why aren't we happy?"[1] While fortunes have dwindled, the question remains: Why, after achieving a certain level of financial stability, does increased wealth not cause increased happiness? Indeed, an additional ten thousand dollars in income is associated with only a 2% increased chance of being happy.[2]

Studies show that irrespective of actual income, most people believe that having roughly 40% more will make them happier.[3] Obviously they can't be right since even people who have that additional income also think they need 40% more. In fact, research indicates that wealth is not a predictor of either happiness or well-being, and furthermore, people who strongly desire wealth are less happy than people who do not.[4] As Robert Kennedy observed,

> The Gross National Product does not allow for the health of our children, the quality of their education, or the joy of their play. It does not include the beauty of our poetry or the strength of our marriages; the intelligence of our public debate or the integrity of our public officials. It measures neither our wit nor our courage; neither our wisdom nor our learning; neither our compassion nor our devotion to our country; it measures everything, in short, except that which makes life worthwhile.[5]

So what makes life worthwhile?

It isn't power, pleasure, financial success, or a focus on self. Of course we want to succeed at something, but success isn't enough. Finding enjoyment in life is essential, but life is about more than enjoyment. In the end, what we really crave more than anything is *significance*. We want our lives to mean something.

A focus on self does not lead to a life of meaning – it is a focus on something greater than self that creates meaning. Whether raising a child, helping a charity, performing public service, or helping those in need, making life better for others is the key to leading a meaningful life.

We know that being kind is good for the people who receive kindness; but when you are kind, it is also good for you. Giving and doing things for others actually lowers the stress hormone associated with unhappiness,[6] and elevates levels of natural opiates known as endorphins. Psychologists call this the "helpers' high."[7] Every type of giving, whether organized or informal – giving to a homeless person, giving to charity, giving blood, even giving directions to lost motorists – are all associated with increased health, happiness, and life satisfaction.[8]

People who give money to nonprofits are 25% more likely to report that their health is either very good or excellent than those who don't give, and those who don't give are about twice as likely to say their health is poor or fair.[9] Volunteering provides similar benefits. In areas as wide ranging as depression relief, weight control, chronic pain reduction, immune functioning, and even indigestion, arthritis, and asthma, the more one volunteers, the greater the health benefits.[10]

Studies also reveal that doing things for others makes us happier. Volunteers and people who give money away are at least 42% more likely to say that they are very happy than those who don't give or volunteer. Conversely, non-givers are about 350% more likely to say they are not happy at all.[11]

Doing things for others also provides financial rewards. Economists have determined that a dollar donated returns about $3.75 in extra income. In fact, on average, a charitable person will earn roughly $14,000 more than a person who doesn't give.[12]

People who do things for others not only become happier and healthier, but so do their friends, and even the friends of their friends, and beyond! Being grateful and kind not only makes you happier, it can make your friends happier, your friends' friends happier, and even their friends happier – happier than an extra $10,000![13]

Writing daily about gratitude and the kind things you do can make you happier, more grateful, more optimistic, kinder, more generous, more satisfied with your life, and even better rested.[14]

Gratitude and a focus on doing things for others are critical elements in a meaningful life. But gratitude is about more than being thankful for what we have. Gratitude is also about being thankful for what we can do for others. All forms of giving are good for us – emotionally, spiritually, and even physically – and everyone has something to give.

How you engage and interact with others is a significant part of how you create who you are – how you become the person you would like to be. When you act like the person you want to be, you transform into that person. Acting grateful makes people more grateful, and acting kind makes people kinder.

Writing about being kind and grateful makes you even kinder and more grateful, which makes your life happier, more satisfying[15] and more meaningful. At the same time, you have a positive effect on people close to you and people you don't even know. Writing about both kindness and gratitude is the key.

An obsessive focus on finding happiness does not make us happy. In fact, happiness is not something we find by searching for it. In our constant quest for wealth and happiness, we have lost sight of what is most important to us – what makes our lives *worthwhile*. Happiness is not found when directly pursued. It is a by-product of a dedication to something greater than ourselves.

For thousands of years, wisdom traditions have taught that gratitude and kindness are necessary for spiritual growth, healthy communities, and finding true happiness. The path to happiness leads through a meaningful life.

It begins with *A Year of Kindness*.

He who wishes to secure the good of others

has already secured his own.

~ Confucius

How to use this journal:

Find today's date, add the year in the blank space, and begin writing. Each page provides a place for writing your thoughts of gratitude, and for recording the kind things you did that day.

If you run out of room on any given day's page, continue in the back of the book on the "carryover" pages. Write the carryover page number where you left off in the parentheses provided.

∽ *For example* ∽

I was about to leave, but (p. 371)

When you have completed the journal, find the page entitled, "My Year of Kindness" (pg. 395) and write your thoughts about your year of journaling about kindness and gratitude.

Don't worry if at first you have a hard time thinking of your kindnesses and things for which you are grateful. It can take a while to get accustomed to thinking and writing about gratitude and daily acts of kindness.

Most importantly, begin today and don't give up!

∽ ∽ ∽

Only a life lived for others is a life worthwhile.

~ *Albert Einstein*

I began my year of kindness on

(date)_____ (year)_____

When you carry out acts of kindness
you get a wonderful feeling inside.
It is as though something inside your
body responds and says, yes, this is
how I ought to feel.

~ Rabbi Harold Kushner

January 1, _____

∾ ∾ ∾

Today I am grateful for:_____

_____

_____

_____

_____

_____ (   )

My Kindnesses today:_____

_____

_____

_____

_____

_____ (   )

∾ ∾ ∾

Today I am grateful for: _____

_____

_____

_____

_____

_____

_____

_____ (   )

My Kindnesses today: _____

_____

_____

_____

_____

_____

_____

_____ (   )

January 3, _____

∾ ∾ ∾

Today I am grateful for: _____

_____

_____

_____

_____

_____

_____

_____ (   )

My Kindnesses today: _____

_____

_____

_____

_____

_____

_____ (   )

Kindness trumps greed:
it asks for sharing.
Kindness trumps fear: it calls forth
gratefulness and love.

~ Marc Estrin

∽ ∽ ∽

Today I am grateful for:_____

_____

_____

_____

_____

_____

_____ (   )

My Kindnesses today:_____

_____

_____

_____

_____

_____ (   )

January 5, _____

∽ ∽ ∽

Today I am grateful for: _____

_____

_____

_____

_____

_____

_____

_____ ( )

My Kindnesses today: _____

_____

_____

_____

_____

_____

_____

_____ ( )

January 6, _____

∾ ∾ ∾

Today I am grateful for:_____

_____

_____

_____

_____

_____

_____

_____ (   )

My Kindnesses today:_____

_____

_____

_____

_____

_____

_____ (   )

January 7, _____

You simply will not be the same person two months from now after consciously giving thanks each day for the abundance that exists in your life. And you will have set in motion an ancient spiritual law: the more you have and are grateful for, the more will be given you.

~ Sarah Ban Breathnach

Today I am grateful for:_____

_____

_____

_____

_____

_____ ( )

My Kindnesses today:_____

_____

_____

_____

_____ ( )

January 8, _____

∾ ∾ ∾

Today I am grateful for: _____

_____

_____

_____

_____

_____

_____

_____ (   )

My Kindnesses today: _____

_____

_____

_____

_____

_____

_____

_____ (   )

January 9, _____

∾ ∾ ∾

Today I am grateful for: _____

_____

_____

_____

_____

_____

_____

_____ ( )

My Kindnesses today: _____

_____

_____

_____

_____

_____

_____ ( )

At times our own light goes out and is rekindled by a spark from another person. Each of us has cause to think with deep gratitude of those who have lighted the flame within us.

~ Albert Schweitzer

∽ ∽ ∽

Today I am grateful for: _____

_____

_____

_____

_____

_____

_____ (   )

My Kindnesses today: _____

_____

_____

_____

_____

_____ (   )

❧ ❧ ❧

Today I am grateful for: _____

_____

_____

_____

_____

_____

_____

_____ ( )

My Kindnesses today: _____

_____

_____

_____

_____

_____

_____

_____ ( )

January 12, _____

∽ ∽ ∽ ∽

Today I am grateful for: _____

_____

_____

_____

_____

_____

_____ ( )

My Kindnesses today: _____

_____

_____

_____

_____

_____

_____ ( )

12

When eating bamboo sprouts,
remember the man who planted them.

~ Chinese Proverb

January 13, _____

೦ ೦ ೦

Today I am grateful for: _____

_____

_____

_____

_____

_____

_____(   )

My Kindnesses today: _____

_____

_____

_____

_____

_____(   )

∾ ∾ ∾

Today I am grateful for: _____

_____

_____

_____

_____

_____

_____ ( )

My Kindnesses today: _____

_____

_____

_____

_____

_____ ( )

January 15, _____

∽ ∽ ∽

Today I am grateful for: _____

_____

_____

_____

_____

_____

_____ (   )

My Kindnesses today: _____

_____

_____

_____

_____

_____

_____ (   )

January 16, _____

People often asked me what is the most effective technique for transforming their life. It is a little embarrassing that after years and years of research and experimentation, I have to say that the best answer is - just be a little kinder.

~ Aldous Huxley

∽ ∾ ∽ ∾

Today I am grateful for: _____

_____

_____

_____

_____

_____ (   )

My Kindnesses today: _____

_____

_____

_____

_____

_____ (   )

∿ ∿ ∿

Today I am grateful for: _____

_____

_____

_____

_____

_____

_____

_____ (   )

My Kindnesses today: _____

_____

_____

_____

_____

_____

_____

_____ (   )

∾ ∾ ∾

Today I am grateful for: _____

_____

_____

_____

_____

_____

_____

_____ ( )

My Kindnesses today: _____

_____

_____

_____

_____

_____

_____ ( )

Let us be grateful to people who make us happy; they are the charming gardeners who make our souls blossom.

~ Marcel Proust

∽ ∽ ∽

Today I am grateful for: _____

_____

_____

_____

_____

_____

_____ ( )

My Kindnesses today: _____

_____

_____

_____

_____

_____ ( )

January 20, _____

∾ ∾ ∾

Today I am grateful for: _____

_____

_____

_____

_____

_____

_____ (   )

My Kindnesses today: _____

_____

_____

_____

_____

_____

_____ (   )

January 21, _____

෴ ෴ ෴

Today I am grateful for: _____

_____

_____

_____

_____

_____

_____

_____ (   )

My Kindnesses today: _____

_____

_____

_____

_____

_____

_____ (   )

If you haven't any charity in your heart,
you have the worst kind of heart trouble.

~ Bob Hope

January 22, _____

❦ ❦ ❦

Today I am grateful for: _____

_____

_____

_____

_____

_____

_____ (   )

My Kindnesses today: _____

_____

_____

_____

_____

_____ (   )

January 23, _____

❧ ❧ ❧

Today I am grateful for: _____

_____

_____

_____

_____

_____

_____

_____ (   )

My Kindnesses today: _____

_____

_____

_____

_____

_____

_____

_____ (   )

January 24, _____

～ ～ ～

Today I am grateful for: _____

_____

_____

_____

_____

_____

_____

_____ (   )

My Kindnesses today: _____

_____

_____

_____

_____

_____

_____ (   )

A life of self-absorption or a life of self-interest would be terribly dull and unsatisfying. I think everyone on some level or other would like to have done something to make the world a better place.

~ Michael Sandel

∽ ∽ ∽

Today I am grateful for: _____

_____

_____

_____

_____

_____

_____ (   )

My Kindnesses today: _____

_____

_____

_____

_____

_____ (   )

January 26, ______

Today I am grateful for: ______________________________

____

____

____

____

____

____

____( )

My Kindnesses today: ______________________________

____

____

____

____

____

____

____( )

∽ ∽ ∽

Today I am grateful for: _____

_____

_____

_____

_____

_____

_____(   )

My Kindnesses today: _____

_____

_____

_____

_____

_____

_____(   )

No act of kindness,
no matter how small, is ever wasted.

~ Aesop

January 28, _____

∾ ∾ ∾

Today I am grateful for: _____

_____

_____

_____

_____

_____

_____ (   )

My Kindnesses today: _____

_____

_____

_____

_____

_____

_____ (   )

28

❧ ❧ ❧

Today I am grateful for: _____

_____

_____

_____

_____

_____

_____ ( )

My Kindnesses today: _____

_____

_____

_____

_____

_____

_____ ( )

∿ ∿ ∿

Today I am grateful for: _____

_____

_____

_____

_____

_____

_____ (   )

My Kindnesses today: _____

_____

_____

_____

_____

_____

_____ (   )

*If you want others to be happy, practice
compassion. If you want to be happy,
practice compassion.*

~ H.H. Dalai Lama

January 31, _____

∞ ∞ ∞

Today I am grateful for: _____

_____

_____

_____

_____

_____ ( )

My Kindnesses today: _____

_____

_____

_____

_____

_____ ( )

∾ ∾ ∾

Today I am grateful for: _____

_____

_____

_____

_____

_____

_____ (   )

My Kindnesses today: _____

_____

_____

_____

_____

_____

_____ (   )

∽ ∽ ∽

Today I am grateful for: _____

_____

_____

_____

_____

_____

_____

_____(   )

My Kindnesses today: _____

_____

_____

_____

_____

_____

_____(   )

He is a wise man who does not grieve
for the things that he has not, but
rejoices for those which he has.
~ Epictetus

February 3, _____

〜 〜 〜

Today I am grateful for: _____

_____

_____

_____

_____

_____

_____ ( )

My Kindnesses today: _____

_____

_____

_____

_____

_____

_____ ( )

February 4, _____

∽ ∽ ∽ ∽

Today I am grateful for: _____

_____

_____

_____

_____

_____

_____

_____ (   )

My Kindnesses today: _____

_____

_____

_____

_____

_____

_____ (   )

February 5, _____

∾ ∾ ∾

Today I am grateful for: _____

_____

_____

_____

_____

_____

_____ (   )

My Kindnesses today: _____

_____

_____

_____

_____

_____

_____ (   )

Wherever there is a human being,
there is an opportunity for a kindness.

~ Seneca

February 6, _____

Today I am grateful for: _____

_____

_____

_____

_____

_____

_____ (   )

My Kindnesses today: _____

_____

_____

_____

_____

_____

_____ (   )

February 7, _____

≈ ≈ ≈

Today I am grateful for: _____

_____

_____

_____

_____

_____

_____

_____ (   )

My Kindnesses today: _____

_____

_____

_____

_____

_____

_____ (   )

February 8, _____

∾ ∾ ∾

Today I am grateful for: _____

_____

_____

_____

_____

_____

_____

_____(   )

My Kindnesses today: _____

_____

_____

_____

_____

_____

_____(   )

We can only be said to be alive in
those moments when our hearts are
conscious of our treasures.

~ Thornton Wilder

∽ ∽ ∽

Today I am grateful for: _____

_____

_____

_____

_____

_____

_____ ( )

My Kindnesses today: _____

_____

_____

_____

_____

_____

_____ ( )

February 10, _____

෴ ෴ ෴

Today I am grateful for: _____

_____

_____

_____

_____

_____

_____

_____(   )

My Kindnesses today: _____

_____

_____

_____

_____

_____

_____(   )

February 11, _____

∽ ∽ ∽

Today I am grateful for: _____

_____

_____

_____

_____

_____

_____

_____ ( )

My Kindnesses today: _____

_____

_____

_____

_____

_____

_____ ( )

42

A kind word is like a Spring day.

~ Russian Proverb

February 12, _____

~ ~ ~

Today I am grateful for: _____

_____

_____

_____

_____

_____ ( )

My Kindnesses today: _____

_____

_____

_____

_____

_____

_____ ( )

February 13, _____

∽ ∽ ∽

Today I am grateful for: _____

_____

_____

_____

_____

_____

_____

_____ (   )

My Kindnesses today: _____

_____

_____

_____

_____

_____

_____

_____ (   )

February 14, _____

∽ ∽ ∽

Today I am grateful for: _____

_____

_____

_____

_____

_____

_____

_____ (   )

My Kindnesses today: _____

_____

_____

_____

_____

_____

_____ (   )

There are only two ways to live your life. One is as though nothing is a miracle. The other is as though everything is a miracle.

~ Albert Einstein

February 15, _____

❧ ❧ ❧

Today I am grateful for: _____

_____

_____

_____

_____

_____ (   )

My Kindnesses today: _____

_____

_____

_____

_____

_____ (   )

∾ ∾ ∾

Today I am grateful for: _____

_____

_____

_____

_____

_____

_____ (   )

My Kindnesses today: _____

_____

_____

_____

_____

_____

_____ (   )

February 17, _____

～ ～ ～

Today I am grateful for: _____

_____

_____

_____

_____

_____

_____ ( )

My Kindnesses today: _____

_____

_____

_____

_____

_____

_____ ( )

48

Kindness is in our power
even when fondness is not.
~ Samuel Johnson

February 18, _____

∾ ∾ ∾

Today I am grateful for: _____

_____

_____

_____

_____

_____

_____ (   )

My Kindnesses today: _____

_____

_____

_____

_____

_____

_____ (   )

49

February 19, _____

∾ ∾ ∾

Today I am grateful for: _____

_____

_____

_____

_____

_____

_____

_____ (   )

My Kindnesses today: _____

_____

_____

_____

_____

_____

_____

_____ (   )

February 20, _____

~ ~ ~

Today I am grateful for: _____

_____

_____

_____

_____

_____

_____ (   )

My Kindnesses today: _____

_____

_____

_____

_____

_____

_____ (   )

Gratitude can transform common days
into thanksgivings, turn routine jobs
into joy, and change ordinary
opportunities into blessings.
~ William Arthur Ward

February 21, _____

෭ ෭ ෭

Today I am grateful for: _____

_____

_____

_____

_____

_____ (   )

My Kindnesses today: _____

_____

_____

_____

_____

_____ (   )

∾ ∾ ∾

Today I am grateful for: _____

_____

_____

_____

_____

_____

_____ (   )

My Kindnesses today: _____

_____

_____

_____

_____

_____

_____ (   )

February 23, _____

~ ~ ~

Today I am grateful for: _____

_____

_____

_____

_____

_____

_____

_____ ( )

My Kindnesses today: _____

_____

_____

_____

_____

_____

_____

_____ ( )

When I was young, I admired
clever people. Now that I am old,
I admire kind people.

~ Abraham Joshua Heschel

February 24, _____

❧ ❧ ❧

Today I am grateful for: _____

_____

_____

_____

_____

_____

_____ (   )

My Kindnesses today: _____

_____

_____

_____

_____

_____ (   )

∾ ∾ ∾

Today I am grateful for: _____

_____

_____

_____

_____

_____

_____

_____ (   )

My Kindnesses today: _____

_____

_____

_____

_____

_____

_____

_____ (   )

February 26, _____

∽ ∾ ∽ ∾ ∽

Today I am grateful for: _____

_____

_____

_____

_____

_____

_____( )

My Kindnesses today: _____

_____

_____

_____

_____

_____

_____( )

Take full account of the excellencies
which you possess, and in gratitude
remember how you would hanker after
them, if you had them not.

~ Marcus Aurelius

February 27, _____

∿ ∿ ∿

Today I am grateful for: _____

_____

_____

_____

_____

_____

_____ (   )

My Kindnesses today: _____

_____

_____

_____

_____

_____ (   )

February 28, _____

∾ ∾ ∾

Today I am grateful for: _____

_____

_____

_____

_____

_____

_____ ( )

My Kindnesses today: _____

_____

_____

_____

_____

_____

_____ ( )

∾ ∾ ∾

Today I am grateful for: _____

_____

_____

_____

_____

_____

_____(   )

My Kindnesses today: _____

_____

_____

_____

_____

_____

_____(   )

You can't live a perfect day without doing something for someone who will never be able to repay you.

~ John Wooden

March 1, _____

∾ ∾ ∾

Today I am grateful for: _____

_____

_____

_____

_____

_____

_____ ( )

My Kindnesses today: _____

_____

_____

_____

_____

_____ ( )

March 2, _____

∾ ∾ ∾

Today I am grateful for: _____

_____

_____

_____

_____

_____

_____ (   )

My Kindnesses today: _____

_____

_____

_____

_____

_____

_____ (   )

March 3, _____

∾ ∾ ∾

Today I am grateful for: _____

_____

_____

_____

_____

_____

_____(   )

My Kindnesses today: _____

_____

_____

_____

_____

_____

_____(   )

We often take for granted the very things that most deserve our gratitude.

~ Cynthia Ozick

March 4, _____

❧ ❧ ❧

Today I am grateful for: _____

_____

_____

_____

_____

_____ (   )

My Kindnesses today: _____

_____

_____

_____

_____

_____

_____ (   )

～ ～ ～

Today I am grateful for: _____

_____

_____

_____

_____

_____

_____

_____ ( )

My Kindnesses today: _____

_____

_____

_____

_____

_____

_____ ( )

∽ ∽ ∽

Today I am grateful for: _____

_____

_____

_____

_____

_____

_____ (   )

My Kindnesses today: _____

_____

_____

_____

_____

_____

_____ (   )

It's a ripple effect that I aspire to.
Hopefully there will be people who say,
"this person made a difference in my life
and it made me act in a different way than
I would have if I had not met this person."

~ Christopher Gergen

∿ ∿ ∿

Today I am grateful for: _____

_____

_____

_____

_____

_____ (   )

My Kindnesses today: _____

_____

_____

_____

_____ (   )

March 8, _____

∾ ∾ ∾

Today I am grateful for: _____

_____

_____

_____

_____

_____

_____

_____(   )

My Kindnesses today: _____

_____

_____

_____

_____

_____

_____(   )

March 9, _____

∽ ∽ ∽

Today I am grateful for: _____

_____

_____

_____

_____

_____

_____

_____ (   )

My Kindnesses today: _____

_____

_____

_____

_____

_____

_____ (   )

If those who owe us nothing gave us
nothing, how poor we would be.

~ Antonio Porchia

March 10, _____

❧ ❧ ❧

Today I am grateful for: _____

_____

_____

_____

_____

_____

_____ (   )

My Kindnesses today: _____

_____

_____

_____

_____

_____

_____

_____ (   )

March 11, _____

∽ ∾ ∽ ∾ ∽ ∾

Today I am grateful for: _____

_____

_____

_____

_____

_____

_____

_____ ( )

My Kindnesses today: _____

_____

_____

_____

_____

_____

_____ ( )

March 12, _____

∾ ∾ ∾

Today I am grateful for: _____

_____

_____

_____

_____

_____

_____

_____ (   )

My Kindnesses today: _____

_____

_____

_____

_____

_____

_____ (   )

When it comes to life, the critical thing
is whether you take things for granted
or take them with gratitude.

~ Gilbert K. Chesterton

March 13, _____

❧ ❧ ❧

Today I am grateful for: _____

_____

_____

_____

_____

_____ (   )

My Kindnesses today: _____

_____

_____

_____

_____

_____ (   )

March 14, _____

❧ ❧ ❧

Today I am grateful for: _____

_____

_____

_____

_____

_____

_____

_____ (   )

My Kindnesses today: _____

_____

_____

_____

_____

_____

_____ (   )

March 15, _____

∾ ∾ ∾

Today I am grateful for: _____

_____

_____

_____

_____

_____

_____ (   )

My Kindnesses today: _____

_____

_____

_____

_____

_____

_____ (   )

March 16, _____

We can be thankful to a friend for a few acres or a little money; and yet for the freedom and command of the whole earth, and for the great benefits of our being, our life, health, and reason, we look upon ourselves as under no obligation.

~ Seneca

～ ～ ～

Today I am grateful for: _____

_____

_____

_____

_____

_____ (   )

My Kindnesses today: _____

_____

_____

_____

_____

_____ (   )

March 17, _____

∾ ∾ ∾

Today I am grateful for: _____

_____

_____

_____

_____

_____

_____ ( )

My Kindnesses today: _____

_____

_____

_____

_____

_____

_____ ( )

March 18, _____

∿ ∿ ∿

Today I am grateful for: _____

_____

_____

_____

_____

_____

_____

_____ (   )

My Kindnesses today: _____

_____

_____

_____

_____

_____

_____ (   )

The best portion of a good man's life —
his little, nameless, unremembered
acts of kindness and love.

~ William Wordsworth

March 19, _____

∽ ∽ ∽

Today I am grateful for: _____

_____

_____

_____

_____

_____ (   )

My Kindnesses today: _____

_____

_____

_____

_____

_____ (   )

March 20, _____

∽ ∽ ∽

Today I am grateful for: _____

_____

_____

_____

_____

_____

_____ ( )

My Kindnesses today: _____

_____

_____

_____

_____

_____

_____ ( )

∽ ∽ ∽

Today I am grateful for: _____

_____

_____

_____

_____

_____

_____ (   )

My Kindnesses today: _____

_____

_____

_____

_____

_____

_____ (   )

March 22, _____

When we become more fully aware that our success is due in large measure to the loyalty, helpfulness, and encouragement we have received from others, our desire grows to pass on similar gifts. Gratitude spurs us on to prove ourselves worthy of what others have done for us. The spirit of gratitude is a powerful energizer.

~ Wilfred A. Peterson

ᘒ ᘒ ᘒ

Today I am grateful for: _____

_____

_____

_____

_____

_____ (   )

My Kindnesses today: _____

_____

_____

_____

_____

_____ (   )

March 23, _____

∾ ∾ ∾

Today I am grateful for: _____

_____

_____

_____

_____

_____

_____ (   )

My Kindnesses today: _____

_____

_____

_____

_____

_____

_____ (   )

March 24, _____

෭ ෭ ෭

Today I am grateful for: _____

_____

_____

_____

_____

_____

_____

_____(   )

My Kindnesses today: _____

_____

_____

_____

_____

_____

_____(   )

Some people have a wonderful capacity
to appreciate again and again,
freshly and naively, the basic goods of
life with awe, pleasure, wonder,
and even ecstasy.

~ A.H. Maslow

∽ ∽ ∽

Today I am grateful for: _____

_____

_____

_____

_____

_____ (   )

My Kindnesses today: _____

_____

_____

_____

_____

_____ (   )

March 26, _____

∽ ∽ ∽ ∽

Today I am grateful for: _____

_____

_____

_____

_____

_____

_____

_____ (   )

My Kindnesses today: _____

_____

_____

_____

_____

_____

_____

_____ (   )

∾ ∾ ∾

Today I am grateful for: _____

_____

_____

_____

_____

_____

_____

_____ (   )

My Kindnesses today: _____

_____

_____

_____

_____

_____

_____ (   )

You cannot do a kindness too soon,

for you never know how soon

it will be too late.

~ Ralph Waldo Emerson

Today I am grateful for: _____

_____

_____

_____

_____

_____

_____ ( )

My Kindnesses today: _____

_____

_____

_____

_____

_____

_____ ( )

∽ ∽ ∽

Today I am grateful for: _____

_____

_____

_____

_____

_____

_____ (   )

My Kindnesses today: _____

_____

_____

_____

_____

_____

_____ (   )

March 30, _____

∽ ∾ ∽ ∾ ∽ ∾

Today I am grateful for: _____

_____

_____

_____

_____

_____

_____

_____ (   )

My Kindnesses today: _____

_____

_____

_____

_____

_____

_____

_____ (   )

March 31, _____

Gratitude unlocks the fullness of life. It turns what we have into enough, and more. It turns denial into acceptance, chaos into order, confusion into clarity…. It turns problems into gifts, failures into success, the unexpected into perfect timing, and mistakes into important events.

~ Melodie Beattie

Today I am grateful for: _____

_____

_____

_____

_____( )

My Kindnesses today: _____

_____

_____

_____

_____( )

April 1, _____

❧ ❧ ❧

Today I am grateful for: _____

_____

_____

_____

_____

_____

_____ ( )

My Kindnesses today: _____

_____

_____

_____

_____

_____

_____ ( )

April 2, _____

∽ ∾ ∽ ∾

Today I am grateful for: _____

_____

_____

_____

_____

_____

_____

_____ (   )

My Kindnesses today: _____

_____

_____

_____

_____

_____

_____

_____ (   )

Be kind, for everyone you meet
is fighting a hard battle.

~ Plato

April 3, _____

❧ ❧ ❧

Today I am grateful for: _____

_____

_____

_____

_____

_____

_____ (   )

My Kindnesses today: _____

_____

_____

_____

_____

_____ (   )

April 4, _____

∾ ∾ ∾

Today I am grateful for: _____

_____

_____

_____

_____

_____

_____

_____ (   )

My Kindnesses today: _____

_____

_____

_____

_____

_____

_____ (   )

95

April 5, _____

෮ ෮ ෮

Today I am grateful for: _____

_____

_____

_____

_____

_____

_____ (   )

My Kindnesses today: _____

_____

_____

_____

_____

_____

_____ (   )

April 6, _____

We should ask ourselves, "What am I trying to accomplish for future generations and for something outside myself?" Self-absorption is often an enemy of getting things done.

~ Jim Woolsey

∾ ∾ ∾

Today I am grateful for: _____

_____

_____

_____

_____

_____ (   )

My Kindnesses today: _____

_____

_____

_____

_____

_____ (   )

April 7, _____

∾ ∾ ∾

Today I am grateful for: _____

_____

_____

_____

_____

_____

_____

_____ (   )

My Kindnesses today: _____

_____

_____

_____

_____

_____

_____ (   )

April 8, _____

∽ ∽ ∽

Today I am grateful for: _____

_____

_____

_____

_____

_____

_____

_____ (   )

My Kindnesses today: _____

_____

_____

_____

_____

_____

_____

_____ (   )

If the only prayer you say in your life
is "thank you," that would suffice.

~ Meister Eckhart

❀ ❀ ❀

Today I am grateful for: _____

_____

_____

_____

_____

_____

_____

_____(   )

My Kindnesses today: _____

_____

_____

_____

_____

_____(   )

April 10, _____

∾ ∾ ∾

Today I am grateful for: _____

_____

_____

_____

_____

_____

_____

_____ (   )

My Kindnesses today: _____

_____

_____

_____

_____

_____

_____ (   )

April 11, _____

∾ ∾ ∾

Today I am grateful for: _____

_____

_____

_____

_____

_____

_____

_____ (   )

My Kindnesses today: _____

_____

_____

_____

_____

_____

_____ (   )

Find the good and praise it.

~ Alex Haley

∾ ∾ ∾

Today I am grateful for: _____

_____

_____

_____

_____

_____

_____ ( )

My Kindnesses today: _____

_____

_____

_____

_____

_____

_____ ( )

April 13, _____

⌒ ⌒ ⌒

Today I am grateful for: _____

_____

_____

_____

_____

_____

_____

_____ (   )

My Kindnesses today: _____

_____

_____

_____

_____

_____

_____ (   )

April 14, _____

∽ ∽ ∽

Today I am grateful for: _____

_____

_____

_____

_____

_____

_____(   )

My Kindnesses today: _____

_____

_____

_____

_____

_____

_____(   )

105

By swallowing evil words unsaid,
no one has ever harmed his stomach.

~ Winston Churchill

April 15, _____

∽ ∽ ∽

Today I am grateful for: _____

_____

_____

_____

_____

_____

_____ ( )

My Kindnesses today: _____

_____

_____

_____

_____

_____ ( )

April 16, _____

∾ ∾ ∾

Today I am grateful for: _____

_____

_____

_____

_____

_____

_____

_____(   )

My Kindnesses today: _____

_____

_____

_____

_____

_____

_____(   )

April 17 _____

∾ ∾ ∾

Today I am grateful for: _____

_____

_____

_____

_____

_____

_____ (   )

My Kindnesses today: _____

_____

_____

_____

_____

_____

_____ (   )

Give thanks for a little
and you will find a lot.

~ The Hausa of Nigeria

April 18, _____

 ✑ ✑ ✑

Today I am grateful for: _____

_____

_____

_____

_____

_____ (   )

My Kindnesses today: _____

_____

_____

_____

_____

_____ (   )

April 19, _____

~ ~ ~

Today I am grateful for: _____

_____

_____

_____

_____

_____

_____ ( )

My Kindnesses today: _____

_____

_____

_____

_____

_____

_____ ( )

April 20, _____

∾ ∾ ∾

Today I am grateful for: _____

_____

_____

_____

_____

_____

_____ (   )

My Kindnesses today: _____

_____

_____

_____

_____

_____

_____ (   )

111

Happiness is itself a kind of gratitude.

~ Joseph Wood Krutch

April 21, _____

∾ ∾ ∾

Today I am grateful for: _____

_____

_____

_____

_____

_____

_____ ( )

My Kindnesses today: _____

_____

_____

_____

_____

_____ ( )

April 22, _____

∽ ∽ ∽

Today I am grateful for: _____

_____

_____

_____

_____

_____

_____

_____ ( )

My Kindnesses today: _____

_____

_____

_____

_____

_____

_____

_____ ( )

April 23, _____

∾ ∾ ∾

Today I am grateful for: _____

_____

_____

_____

_____

_____

_____ ( )

My Kindnesses today: _____

_____

_____

_____

_____

_____

_____ ( )

April 24, _____

Remember there's no such thing as a
small act of kindness. Every act
creates a ripple with no logical end.

~ Scott Adams

ॐ ॐ ॐ

Today I am grateful for: _____

_____

_____

_____

_____

_____

_____ (   )

My Kindnesses today: _____

_____

_____

_____

_____

_____ (   )

April 25, _____

～ ～ ～

Today I am grateful for: _____

_____

_____

_____

_____

_____

_____ (   )

My Kindnesses today: _____

_____

_____

_____

_____

_____

_____ (   )

∽ ∽ ∽

Today I am grateful for: _____

_____

_____

_____

_____

_____

_____ (   )

My Kindnesses today: _____

_____

_____

_____

_____

_____

_____ (   )

Real generosity is doing something nice
for someone who will never find out.

~ Frank A. Clark

April 27, _____

∽ ∽ ∽

Today I am grateful for: _____

_____

_____

_____

_____

_____

_____ ( )

My Kindnesses today: _____

_____

_____

_____

_____

_____ ( )

April 28, _____

∽ ∽ ∽

Today I am grateful for: _____

_____

_____

_____

_____

_____

_____ ( )

My Kindnesses today: _____

_____

_____

_____

_____

_____

_____ ( )

April 29, _____

~ ~ ~

Today I am grateful for: _____

_____

_____

_____

_____

_____

_____ (   )

My Kindnesses today: _____

_____

_____

_____

_____

_____

_____ (   )

April 30, _____

*I think the most fulfilling thing is
when you can do something that brings
happiness to a bunch of other people.*

~ *Bill Budinger*

❧ ❧ ❧

Today I am grateful for: _____

_____

_____

_____

_____

_____

_____ ( )

My Kindnesses today: _____

_____

_____

_____

_____

_____

_____ ( )

May 1, _____

∽ ∽ ∽

Today I am grateful for: _____

_____

_____

_____

_____

_____

_____

_____ (   )

My Kindnesses today: _____

_____

_____

_____

_____

_____

_____

_____ (   )

May 2, _____

∽ ∾ ∽

Today I am grateful for: _____

_____

_____

_____

_____

_____

_____

_____ (   )

My Kindnesses today: _____

_____

_____

_____

_____

_____

_____

_____ (   )

There is a calmness to a life
lived in gratitude, a quiet joy.

~ Ralph H. Blum

May 3, _____

❧ ❧ ❧

Today I am grateful for: _____

_____

_____

_____

_____

_____

_____ ( )

My Kindnesses today: _____

_____

_____

_____

_____

_____ ( )

May 4, _____

∾ ∾ ∾

Today I am grateful for: _____

_____

_____

_____

_____

_____

_____

_____ (   )

My Kindnesses today: _____

_____

_____

_____

_____

_____

_____

_____ (   )

May 5, _____

∽ ∽ ∽

Today I am grateful for: _____

_____

_____

_____

_____

_____

_____

_____ ( )

My Kindnesses today: _____

_____

_____

_____

_____

_____

_____

_____ ( )

Gratefulness is the key to a happy life that we hold in our hands, because if we are not grateful, then no matter how much we have we will not be happy — because we will always want to have something else or something more.

~ Brother David Steindl-Rast

∽ ∽ ∽

Today I am grateful for: _____

_____

_____

_____

_____

_____ (   )

My Kindnesses today: _____

_____

_____

_____

_____

_____ (   )

May 7, _____

❧ ❧ ❧

Today I am grateful for: _____

_____

_____

_____

_____

_____

_____

_____ (   )

My Kindnesses today: _____

_____

_____

_____

_____

_____

_____

_____ (   )

May 8, _____

∽ ∽ ∽

Today I am grateful for: _____

_____

_____

_____

_____

_____

_____( )

My Kindnesses today: _____

_____

_____

_____

_____

_____

_____( )

If we pursue success directly, it will
elude us. If we pursue significance, if we
do things that are other-regarding,
if we do things of significance, then
I think success will come.

~ Dov Seidman

May 9, _____

Today I am grateful for: _____

_____

_____

_____

_____

_____ ( )

My Kindnesses today: _____

_____

_____

_____

_____

_____ ( )

May 10, _____

～ ～ ～

Today I am grateful for: _____

_____

_____

_____

_____

_____

_____

_____ ( )

My Kindnesses today: _____

_____

_____

_____

_____

_____

_____

_____ ( )

May 11, _____

∼ ∼ ∼

Today I am grateful for: _____

_____

_____

_____

_____

_____

_____

_____ (   )

My Kindnesses today: _____

_____

_____

_____

_____

_____

_____ (   )

Being considerate of others
will take your children further in life
than any college degree.

~ Marian Wright Edelman

May 12, _____

∾ ∾ ∾

Today I am grateful for: _____

_____

_____

_____

_____

_____

_____ (   )

My Kindnesses today: _____

_____

_____

_____

_____

_____

_____ (   )

May 13, _____

∽ ∽ ∽

Today I am grateful for: _____

_____

_____

_____

_____

_____

_____ (   )

My Kindnesses today: _____

_____

_____

_____

_____

_____

_____ (   )

134

~ ~ ~

Today I am grateful for: _____

_____

_____

_____

_____

_____

_____ (   )

My Kindnesses today: _____

_____

_____

_____

_____

_____

_____ (   )

Happiness cannot be traveled to, owned, earned, worn or consumed. Happiness is the spiritual experience of living every minute with love, grace and gratitude.

~ Denis Waitley

May 15, _____

Today I am grateful for: _____

_____

_____

_____

_____

_____ ( )

My Kindnesses today: _____

_____

_____

_____

_____

_____

_____ ( )

May 16, _____

∽ ∽ ∽

Today I am grateful for: _____

_____

_____

_____

_____

_____

_____ ( )

My Kindnesses today: _____

_____

_____

_____

_____

_____

_____ ( )

∾ ∾ ∾

Today I am grateful for: _____

_____

_____

_____

_____

_____

_____

_____ (   )

My Kindnesses today: _____

_____

_____

_____

_____

_____

_____

_____ (   )

May 18, _____

Too often we underestimate the power of a touch, a smile, a kind word, a listening ear, an honest compliment, or the smallest act of caring, all of which have the potential to turn a life around.

~ Leo Buscaglia

೦ ೦ ೦

Today I am grateful for: _____

_____

_____

_____

_____

_____ (   )

My Kindnesses today: _____

_____

_____

_____

_____

_____ (   )

May 19, _____

෧ ෧ ෧

Today I am grateful for: _____

_____

_____

_____

_____

_____

_____

_____ (   )

My Kindnesses today: _____

_____

_____

_____

_____

_____

_____ (   )

∽ ∽ ∽

Today I am grateful for: _____

_____

_____

_____

_____

_____

_____ (   )

My Kindnesses today: _____

_____

_____

_____

_____

_____

_____ (   )

Kindness is the highest wisdom.

~ Gilbert Milton Kotzen

May 21, _____

∾ ∾ ∾

Today I am grateful for: _____

_____

_____

_____

_____

_____

_____

_____ (   )

My Kindnesses today: _____

_____

_____

_____

_____

_____

_____ (   )

May 22, _____

∽ ∽ ∽

Today I am grateful for: _____

_____

_____

_____

_____

_____

_____(   )

My Kindnesses today: _____

_____

_____

_____

_____

_____

_____(   )

May 23, _____

∽ ∽ ∽

Today I am grateful for: _____

_____

_____

_____

_____

_____

_____

_____ (   )

My Kindnesses today: _____

_____

_____

_____

_____

_____

_____ (   )

A bit of fragrance always clings
to the hand that gives roses.

~ Chinese Proverb

~ ~ ~

Today I am grateful for: _____

_____

_____

_____

_____

_____

_____

_____ (   )

My Kindnesses today: _____

_____

_____

_____

_____

_____ (   )

May 25, _____

∾ ∾ ∾

Today I am grateful for: _____

_____

_____

_____

_____

_____

_____ (   )

My Kindnesses today: _____

_____

_____

_____

_____

_____

_____ (   )

May 26, _____

∽ ∽ ∽

Today I am grateful for: _____

_____

_____

_____

_____

_____

_____

_____ (   )

My Kindnesses today: _____

_____

_____

_____

_____

_____

_____

_____ (   )

A person who is nice to you but rude to

the waiter is not a nice person.

~ Dave Barry

May 27, _____

∾ ∾ ∾

Today I am grateful for: _____

_____

_____

_____

_____

_____

_____ (   )

My Kindnesses today: _____

_____

_____

_____

_____

_____

_____

_____ (   )

May 28, _____

∾ ∾ ∾

Today I am grateful for: _____

_____

_____

_____

_____

_____

_____ (   )

My Kindnesses today: _____

_____

_____

_____

_____

_____

_____ (   )

Without gratitude you cannot long
keep from dissatisfied thought
regarding things as they are.

~ Wallace Wattles

May 29, _____

∾ ∾ ∾

Today I am grateful for: _____

_____

_____

_____

_____

_____

_____ (   )

My Kindnesses today: _____

_____

_____

_____

_____

_____

_____ (   )

May 30, _____

∽ ∽ ∽

Today I am grateful for: _____

_____

_____

_____

_____

_____

_____

_____ (   )

My Kindnesses today: _____

_____

_____

_____

_____

_____

_____

_____ (   )

*Life is short
but there is always time for courtesy.*

~ Ralph Waldo Emerson

May 31, _____

೦೨ ೦೨ ೦೨

Today I am grateful for: _____

_____

_____

_____

_____

_____

_____ (   )

My Kindnesses today: _____

_____

_____

_____

_____

_____ (   )

∾ ∾ ∾

Today I am grateful for: _____

_____

_____

_____

_____

_____

_____

_____ (   )

My Kindnesses today: _____

_____

_____

_____

_____

_____

_____ (   )

June 2, _____

∾ ∾ ∾

Today I am grateful for: _____

_____

_____

_____

_____

_____

_____ (   )

My Kindnesses today: _____

_____

_____

_____

_____

_____

_____ (   )

We really do have an opportunity to make a contribution. We can work together to change our conditions. There are so many ways that you can make a difference.

~ Kathleen Kennedy Townsend

June 3, _____

∽ ∽ ∽

Today I am grateful for: _____

_____

_____

_____

_____

_____ (   )

My Kindnesses today: _____

_____

_____

_____

_____

_____ (   )

June 4, _____

∽ ∽ ∽

Today I am grateful for: _____

_____

_____

_____

_____

_____

_____

_____(   )

My Kindnesses today: _____

_____

_____

_____

_____

_____

_____

_____(   )

June 5, _____

∽ ∽ ∽

Today I am grateful for: _____

_____

_____

_____

_____

_____

_____ ( )

My Kindnesses today: _____

_____

_____

_____

_____

_____

_____ ( )

June 6, _____

If you concentrate on finding whatever is good in every situation,
you will discover that your life will suddenly be filled with gratitude,
a feeling that nurtures the soul.

~ Rabbi Harold Kushner

∽ ∽ ∽

Today I am grateful for: _____

_____

_____

_____

_____

_____ (   )

My Kindnesses today: _____

_____

_____

_____

_____

_____ (   )

∿ ∿ ∿

Today I am grateful for: _____

_____

_____

_____

_____

_____

_____ (   )

My Kindnesses today: _____

_____

_____

_____

_____

_____

_____ (   )

June 8, _____

❀ ❀ ❀

Today I am grateful for: _____

_____

_____

_____

_____

_____

_____ ( )

My Kindnesses today: _____

_____

_____

_____

_____

_____

_____ ( )

To cultivate kindness is a valuable part
of the business of life.

Samuel Johnson

∾ ∾ ∾

Today I am grateful for: _____

_____

_____

_____

_____

_____

_____ ( )

My Kindnesses today: _____

_____

_____

_____

_____

_____

_____ ( )

∾ ∾ ∾

Today I am grateful for: _____

_____

_____

_____

_____

_____

_____ (   )

My Kindnesses today: _____

_____

_____

_____

_____

_____

_____ (   )

∽ ∽ ∽

Today I am grateful for: _____

_____

_____

_____

_____

_____

_____ ( )

My Kindnesses today: _____

_____

_____

_____

_____

_____

_____ ( )

Nothing that is done for you is a matter of course.

Everything originates in a will for the good which is directed at you.

Train yourself never to put off the word or action

for the expression of gratitude.

~ Albert Schweitzer

∾ ∾ ∾

Today I am grateful for: _____

_____

_____

_____

_____

_____ (   )

My Kindnesses today: _____

_____

_____

_____

_____

_____ (   )

June 13, _____

∾ ∾ ∾

Today I am grateful for: _____

_____

_____

_____

_____

_____

_____ ( )

My Kindnesses today: _____

_____

_____

_____

_____

_____

_____ ( )

June 14, _____

∽ ∽ ∽ ∽

Today I am grateful for: _____

_____

_____

_____

_____

_____

_____

_____ (   )

My Kindnesses today: _____

_____

_____

_____

_____

_____

_____

_____ (   )

The more sympathy you give,
the less you need.

~ Malcolm S. Forbes

June 15, _____

∾ ∾ ∾

Today I am grateful for: _____

_____

_____

_____

_____

_____

_____ (   )

My Kindnesses today: _____

_____

_____

_____

_____

_____ (   )

June 16, _____

∽ ∽ ∽

Today I am grateful for: _____

_____

_____

_____

_____

_____

_____

_____(   )

My Kindnesses today: _____

_____

_____

_____

_____

_____

_____(   )

June 17, _____

∽ ∽ ∽

Today I am grateful for: _____

_____

_____

_____

_____

_____

_____

_____ (   )

My Kindnesses today: _____

_____

_____

_____

_____

_____

_____

_____ (   )

God gave you a gift of
86,400 seconds today.
Have you used one to say "thank you?"

~ William A. Ward

∽ ∽ ∽

Today I am grateful for: _____

_____

_____

_____

_____

_____

_____ ( )

My Kindnesses today: _____

_____

_____

_____

_____

_____ ( )

170

June 19, _____

～ ～ ～

Today I am grateful for: _____

_____

_____

_____

_____

_____

_____

_____ (   )

My Kindnesses today: _____

_____

_____

_____

_____

_____

_____ (   )

171

June 20, _____

∾ ∾ ∾

Today I am grateful for: _____

_____

_____

_____

_____

_____

_____

_____ (   )

My Kindnesses today: _____

_____

_____

_____

_____

_____

_____

_____ (   )

Gratitude is a vaccine,

an antitoxin, and an antiseptic.

~ John Henry Jowett

෨ ෨ ෨

Today I am grateful for: _____

_____

_____

_____

_____

_____

_____ ( )

My Kindnesses today: _____

_____

_____

_____

_____

_____ ( )

June 22, _____

∾ ∾ ∾

Today I am grateful for: _____

_____

_____

_____

_____

_____

_____

_____ (   )

My Kindnesses today: _____

_____

_____

_____

_____

_____

_____

_____ (   )

June 23, _____

∽ ∽ ∽

Today I am grateful for: _____

_____

_____

_____

_____

_____

_____ (   )

My Kindnesses today: _____

_____

_____

_____

_____

_____

_____ (   )

Reflect upon your present blessings,

of which every man has plenty;

not on your past misfortunes,

of which all men have some.

~ Charles Dickens

Today I am grateful for: _____

_____

_____

_____

_____

_____ (   )

My Kindnesses today: _____

_____

_____

_____

_____

_____ (   )

∾ ∾ ∾

Today I am grateful for: _____

_____

_____

_____

_____

_____

_____

_____ (   )

My Kindnesses today: _____

_____

_____

_____

_____

_____

_____ (   )

∾ ∾ ∾

Today I am grateful for: _____

_____

_____

_____

_____

_____

_____

_____ (   )

My Kindnesses today: _____

_____

_____

_____

_____

_____

_____ (   )

In about the same degree as you are helpful,

you will be happy.

~ Karl Reiland

June 27, _____

❧ ❧ ❧

Today I am grateful for: _____

_____

_____

_____

_____

_____

_____

_____ ( )

My Kindnesses today: _____

_____

_____

_____

_____

_____ ( )

∽ ∽ ∽

Today I am grateful for: _____

_____

_____

_____

_____

_____

_____

_____(   )

My Kindnesses today: _____

_____

_____

_____

_____

_____

_____(   )

❧ ❧ ❧

Today I am grateful for: _____

_____

_____

_____

_____

_____

_____ (   )

My Kindnesses today: _____

_____

_____

_____

_____

_____

_____ (   )

Whenever we are appreciative, we are
filled with a sense of well being
and swept up by the feeling of joy.

~ M.J. Ryan

∽ ∽ ∽

Today I am grateful for: _____

_____

_____

_____

_____

_____ (   )

My Kindnesses today: _____

_____

_____

_____

_____

_____ (   )

July 1, _____

~ ~ ~

Today I am grateful for: _____

_____

_____

_____

_____

_____

_____

_____ (   )

My Kindnesses today: _____

_____

_____

_____

_____

_____

_____

_____ (   )

∽ ∽ ∽

Today I am grateful for: _____

_____

_____

_____

_____

_____

_____

_____ (   )

My Kindnesses today: _____

_____

_____

_____

_____

_____

_____ (   )

July 3, _____

I expect to pass through life but once. If therefore, there be any kindness
I can show, or any good thing I can do to any fellow being, let me do it now,
and not defer or neglect it, as I shall not pass this way again.

~ William Penn

∾ ∾ ∾

Today I am grateful for: _____

_____

_____

_____

_____

_____ (   )

My Kindnesses today: _____

_____

_____

_____

_____

_____ (   )

July 4, _____

∽ ∽ ∽

Today I am grateful for: _____

_____

_____

_____

_____

_____

_____ (   )

My Kindnesses today: _____

_____

_____

_____

_____

_____

_____ (   )

July 5, _____

～ ～ ～

Today I am grateful for: _____

_____

_____

_____

_____

_____

_____ (   )

My Kindnesses today: _____

_____

_____

_____

_____

_____

_____ (   )

Gratitude is riches.

Complaint is poverty.

~ Doris Day

∽ ∽ ∽

Today I am grateful for: _____

_____

_____

_____

_____

_____

_____ (   )

My Kindnesses today: _____

_____

_____

_____

_____

_____ (   )

≈ ≈ ≈

Today I am grateful for: _____

_____

_____

_____

_____

_____

_____

_____ (   )

My Kindnesses today: _____

_____

_____

_____

_____

_____

_____ (   )

189

A life devoted only to self
is a life not lived to the fullest.

William A. Haseltine

July 8, _____

Today I am grateful for: _____

_____

_____

_____

_____

_____

_____ (   )

My Kindnesses today: _____

_____

_____

_____

_____

_____ (   )

∽ ∽ ∽

Today I am grateful for: _____

_____

_____

_____

_____

_____

_____

_____ (   )

My Kindnesses today: _____

_____

_____

_____

_____

_____

_____ (   )

July 10, _____

∿ ∿ ∿

Today I am grateful for: _____

_____

_____

_____

_____

_____

_____

_____ (   )

My Kindnesses today: _____

_____

_____

_____

_____

_____

_____ (   )

The greatest good you can do for
another is not just to share your riches
but to reveal to him his own.

~ Benjamin Disraeli

July 11, _____

∾ ∾ ∾

Today I am grateful for: _____

_____

_____

_____

_____

_____

_____ (   )

My Kindnesses today: _____

_____

_____

_____

_____

_____

_____ (   )

July 12, _____

～ ～ ～

Today I am grateful for: _____

_____

_____

_____

_____

_____

_____

_____ (   )

My Kindnesses today: _____

_____

_____

_____

_____

_____

_____ (   )

July 13, _____

෮ ෮ ෮

Today I am grateful for: _____

_____

_____

_____

_____

_____

_____ ( )

My Kindnesses today: _____

_____

_____

_____

_____

_____

_____ ( )

Many people who order their lives rightly in all other ways are kept in poverty by their lack of gratitude.

~ Wallace Wattles

July 14, _____

ᖇ ᖇ ᖇ

Today I am grateful for: _____

_____

_____

_____

_____

_____ (   )

My Kindnesses today: _____

_____

_____

_____

_____

_____ (   )

July 15, _____

∾ ∾ ∾

Today I am grateful for: _____

_____

_____

_____

_____

_____

_____

_____ (   )

My Kindnesses today: _____

_____

_____

_____

_____

_____

_____ (   )

July 16, _____

∽ ∾ ∽ ∾ ∽ ∾

Today I am grateful for: _____

_____

_____

_____

_____

_____

_____

_____ (   )

My Kindnesses today: _____

_____

_____

_____

_____

_____

_____ (   )

How beautiful a day can be
when kindness touches it!

~ George Elliston

July 17, _____

❧ ❧ ❧

Today I am grateful for: _____

_____

_____

_____

_____

_____

_____ (   )

My Kindnesses today: _____

_____

_____

_____

_____

_____ (   )

∽ ∽ ∽

Today I am grateful for: _____

_____

_____

_____

_____

_____

_____

_____ ( )

My Kindnesses today: _____

_____

_____

_____

_____

_____

_____ ( )

July 19, _____

∽ ∽ ∽

Today I am grateful for: _____

_____

_____

_____

_____

_____

_____(   )

My Kindnesses today: _____

_____

_____

_____

_____

_____

_____(   )

July 20, _____

Let us rise up and be thankful, for if we didn't learn a lot today,
at least we learned a little, and if we didn't learn a little, at least we didn't get sick,
and if we got sick, at least we didn't die; so, let us all be thankful.

~ The Buddha

∾ ∾ ∾ ∾

Today I am grateful for: _____

_____

_____

_____

_____

_____ (   )

My Kindnesses today: _____

_____

_____

_____

_____

_____ (   )

July 21, _____

≈ ≈ ≈

Today I am grateful for: _____

_____

_____

_____

_____

_____

_____

_____ (   )

My Kindnesses today: _____

_____

_____

_____

_____

_____

_____

_____ (   )

203

July 22, _____

∽ ∽ ∽

Today I am grateful for: _____

_____

_____

_____

_____

_____

_____(   )

My Kindnesses today: _____

_____

_____

_____

_____

_____

_____(   )

We are made kind by being kind.

~ Eric Hoffer

July 23, _____

∾ ∾ ∾

Today I am grateful for: _____

_____

_____

_____

_____

_____ (   )

My Kindnesses today: _____

_____

_____

_____

_____ (   )

July 24, _____

∿ ∿ ∿

Today I am grateful for: _____

_____

_____

_____

_____

_____

_____( )

My Kindnesses today: _____

_____

_____

_____

_____

_____

_____( )

July 25, _____

❧ ❧ ❧

Today I am grateful for: _____

_____

_____

_____

_____

_____

_____(   )

My Kindnesses today: _____

_____

_____

_____

_____

_____

_____(   )

Two kinds of gratitude:
The sudden kind we feel for what we take;
the larger kind we feel for what we give.

~ Edwin Arlington Robinson

July 26, _____

∽ ∽ ∽

Today I am grateful for: _____

_____

_____

_____

_____

_____

_____( )

My Kindnesses today: _____

_____

_____

_____

_____

_____

_____( )

July 27, _____

∽ ∽ ∽

Today I am grateful for: _____

_____

_____

_____

_____

_____

_____ (   )

My Kindnesses today: _____

_____

_____

_____

_____

_____

_____ (   )

July 28, _____

~ ~ ~

Today I am grateful for: _____

_____

_____

_____

_____

_____

_____ ( )

My Kindnesses today: _____

_____

_____

_____

_____

_____

_____ ( )

July 29, _____

Have you done the right thing in your own life and have you treated people well? What do you want to do tomorrow that will make the world a better place? Because when you leave this world, people are probably not going to remember you. So what is it?

~ Gay MacGregor

᷒ ᷒ ᷒

Today I am grateful for: _____

_____

_____

_____

_____ ( )

My Kindnesses today: _____

_____

_____

_____

_____ ( )

∾ ∾ ∾

Today I am grateful for: _____

_____

_____

_____

_____

_____

_____

_____ ( )

My Kindnesses today: _____

_____

_____

_____

_____

_____

_____ ( )

July 31, _____

～ ～ ～

Today I am grateful for: _____

_____

_____

_____

_____

_____

_____

_____ ( )

My Kindnesses today: _____

_____

_____

_____

_____

_____

_____

_____ ( )

Kindness is the golden chain by which society is bound together.

~ Goethe

August 1, _____

Today I am grateful for: _____

_____

_____

_____

_____

_____

_____ (   )

My Kindnesses today: _____

_____

_____

_____

_____

_____ (   )

August 2, _____

Today I am grateful for: _____

_____

_____

_____

_____

_____

_____ (   )

My Kindnesses today: _____

_____

_____

_____

_____

_____

_____ (   )

215

August 3, _____

∽ ∽ ∽

Today I am grateful for: _____

_____

_____

_____

_____

_____

_____ ( )

My Kindnesses today: _____

_____

_____

_____

_____

_____

_____ ( )

Start bringing gratitude to your experiences instead of waiting for a positive experience in order to feel grateful. Gratitude should not be just a reaction to getting what you want, but an all-the-time gratitude, the kind where you notice the little things and where you constantly look for the good, even in unpleasant situations.

~ Marelisa Fábrega

Today I am grateful for: _____

_____

_____

_____

_____

_____ (   )

My Kindnesses today: _____

_____

_____

_____

_____

_____ (   )

August 5, _____

∾ ∾ ∾

Today I am grateful for: _____

_____

_____

_____

_____

_____

_____

_____ (   )

My Kindnesses today: _____

_____

_____

_____

_____

_____

_____

_____ (   )

August 6, _____

∾ ∾ ∾

Today I am grateful for: _____

_____

_____

_____

_____

_____

_____ (   )

My Kindnesses today: _____

_____

_____

_____

_____

_____

_____ (   )

When we feel love and kindness toward
others, it not only makes others feel
loved and cared for, but it helps us also
to develop inner happiness and peace.

~ H.H. Dalai Lama

∾ ∾ ∾

Today I am grateful for: _____

_____

_____

_____

_____

_____ (   )

My Kindnesses today: _____

_____

_____

_____

_____

_____

_____ (   )

August 8, _____

∽ ∽ ∽

Today I am grateful for: _____

_____

_____

_____

_____

_____

_____

_____ (   )

My Kindnesses today: _____

_____

_____

_____

_____

_____

_____

_____ (   )

August 9, _____

∽ ∽ ∽

Today I am grateful for: _____

_____

_____

_____

_____

_____

_____ (   )

My Kindnesses today: _____

_____

_____

_____

_____

_____ (   )

August 10, _____

Teach this triple truth to all:
A generous heart, kind speech,
and a life of service and compassion
are the things that renew humanity.

~ Buddha

∽ ∽ ∽

Today I am grateful for: _____

_____

_____

_____

_____

_____( )

My Kindnesses today: _____

_____

_____

_____

_____

_____( )

August 11, _____

∾ ∾ ∾

Today I am grateful for: _____

_____

_____

_____

_____

_____

_____

_____ (   )

My Kindnesses today: _____

_____

_____

_____

_____

_____

_____ (   )

August 12, _____

~ ~ ~

Today I am grateful for: _____

_____

_____

_____

_____

_____

_____

_____ (   )

My Kindnesses today: _____

_____

_____

_____

_____

_____

_____ (   )

Saying thank you is more than good

manners. It is good spirituality.

~ Alfred Painter

August 13, _____

∾ ∾ ∾

Today I am grateful for: _____

_____

_____

_____

_____

_____ ( )

My Kindnesses today: _____

_____

_____

_____

_____

_____ ( )

August 14, _____

∽ ∽ ∽

Today I am grateful for: _____

_____

_____

_____

_____

_____

_____

_____ (   )

My Kindnesses today: _____

_____

_____

_____

_____

_____

_____

_____ (   )

August 15, _____

∽ ∾ ∽ ∾ ∽ ∾

Today I am grateful for: _____

_____

_____

_____

_____

_____

_____

_____ ( )

My Kindnesses today: _____

_____

_____

_____

_____

_____

_____ ( )

Gratitude is not only the greatest of virtues,
but the parent of all the others.

~ Cicero

August 16, _____

∽ ∽ ∽

Today I am grateful for: _____

_____

_____

_____

_____

_____ (   )

My Kindnesses today: _____

_____

_____

_____

_____

_____ (   )

August 17, _____

∾ ∾ ∾

Today I am grateful for: _____

_____

_____

_____

_____

_____

_____

_____ (   )

My Kindnesses today: _____

_____

_____

_____

_____

_____

_____ (   )

August 18, _____

∽ ∽ ∽

Today I am grateful for: _____

_____

_____

_____

_____

_____

_____ (   )

My Kindnesses today: _____

_____

_____

_____

_____

_____

_____ (   )

The hardest arithmetic to master

is that which enables us

to count our blessings.

~ Eric Hoffer

August 19, _____

ல ல ல

Today I am grateful for: _____

_____

_____

_____

_____

_____ ( )

My Kindnesses today: _____

_____

_____

_____

_____

_____ ( )

∽ ∾ ∽

Today I am grateful for: _____

_____

_____

_____

_____

_____

_____

_____ ( )

My Kindnesses today: _____

_____

_____

_____

_____

_____

_____ ( )

∾ ∾ ∾

Today I am grateful for: _____

_____

_____

_____

_____

_____

_____

_____ (   )

My Kindnesses today: _____

_____

_____

_____

_____

_____

_____ (   )

There is nothing better than
the encouragement of a good friend.
~ Katharine Butler Hathaway

August 22, _____

❧ ❧ ❧

Today I am grateful for: _____

_____

_____

_____

_____

_____ ( )

My Kindnesses today: _____

_____

_____

_____

_____

_____ ( )

August 23, _____

∾ ∾ ∾

Today I am grateful for: _____

_____

_____

_____

_____

_____

_____ ( )

My Kindnesses today: _____

_____

_____

_____

_____

_____

_____ ( )

August 24, _____

∽ ∽ ∽

Today I am grateful for: _____

_____

_____

_____

_____

_____

_____ (   )

My Kindnesses today: _____

_____

_____

_____

_____

_____

_____ (   )

Gratitude is the fairest blossom
which springs from the soul.
~ Henry Ward Beecher

August 25, _____

∽ ∽ ∽

Today I am grateful for: _____

_____

_____

_____

_____

_____

_____ (   )

My Kindnesses today: _____

_____

_____

_____

_____

_____ (   )

∾ ∾ ∾

Today I am grateful for: _____

_____

_____

_____

_____

_____

_____

_____(   )

My Kindnesses today: _____

_____

_____

_____

_____

_____

_____(   )

August 27, _____

∾ ∾ ∾

Today I am grateful for: _____

_____

_____

_____

_____

_____

_____ (   )

My Kindnesses today: _____

_____

_____

_____

_____

_____

_____ (   )

August 28, _____

*If you can look back on your life and say that because I lived my life in a certain way that changed some people for the better or changed the world for the better or changed some people's lives and experiences for the better...
well, that is something worth looking back on.*

~ Shashi Tharoor

∾ ∾ ∾

Today I am grateful for: _____

_____

_____

_____

_____ ( )

My Kindnesses today: _____

_____

_____

_____

_____ ( )

August 29, _____

～ ～ ～

Today I am grateful for: _____

_____

_____

_____

_____

_____

_____ (   )

My Kindnesses today: _____

_____

_____

_____

_____

_____

_____ (   )

August 30, _____

∾ ∾ ∾

Today I am grateful for: _____

_____

_____

_____

_____

_____

_____

_____ (   )

My Kindnesses today: _____

_____

_____

_____

_____

_____

_____ (   )

Don't pray when it rains if you don't
pray when the sun shines.
~ Satchel Paige

August 31, _____

ᔭ ᔭ ᔭ

Today I am grateful for: _____

_____

_____

_____

_____

_____

_____ (   )

My Kindnesses today: _____

_____

_____

_____

_____

_____

_____ (   )

September 1, _____

∾ ∾ ∾

Today I am grateful for: _____

_____

_____

_____

_____

_____

_____(   )

My Kindnesses today: _____

_____

_____

_____

_____

_____

_____(   )

September 2, _____

∿ ∿ ∿

Today I am grateful for: _____

_____

_____

_____

_____

_____

_____ ( )

My Kindnesses today: _____

_____

_____

_____

_____

_____ ( )

*My mother always said to
leave the world a little better than
it was when we arrived.*

~ Judith Reisman

September 3, _____

∾ ∾ ∾

Today I am grateful for: _____

_____

_____

_____

_____

_____ (   )

My Kindnesses today: _____

_____

_____

_____

_____

_____ (   )

September 4, _____

∽ ∽ ∽

Today I am grateful for: _____

_____

_____

_____

_____

_____

_____ (   )

My Kindnesses today: _____

_____

_____

_____

_____

_____

_____ (   )

September 5, _____

∽ ∽ ∽

Today I am grateful for: _____

_____

_____

_____

_____

_____

_____

_____ ( )

My Kindnesses today: _____

_____

_____

_____

_____

_____

_____ ( )

To speak gratitude is courteous and pleasant,

to enact gratitude is generous and noble,

but to live gratitude is to touch Heaven.

~ Johannes A. Gaertner

September 6, _____

❧ ❧ ❧

Today I am grateful for: _____

_____

_____

_____

_____

_____ (   )

My Kindnesses today: _____

_____

_____

_____

_____

_____

_____ (   )

September 7, _____

∽ ∽ ∽

Today I am grateful for: _____

_____

_____

_____

_____

_____

_____

_____ (   )

My Kindnesses today: _____

_____

_____

_____

_____

_____

_____ (   )

September 8, _____

～ ～ ～

Today I am grateful for: _____

_____

_____

_____

_____

_____

_____

_____ (   )

My Kindnesses today: _____

_____

_____

_____

_____

_____

_____ (   )

Think about what you did today and what you will do the next day to make sure
that you are helping others - that you live a life worth living.
When you go to sleep at night, you will have a good feeling.
~ Rabbi Menachem Mendel Mintz

∾ ∾ ∾

Today I am grateful for: _____

_____

_____

_____

_____ (   )

My Kindnesses today: _____

_____

_____

_____

_____ (   )

September 10, _____

∽ ∽ ∽

Today I am grateful for: _____

_____

_____

_____

_____

_____

_____ (   )

My Kindnesses today: _____

_____

_____

_____

_____

_____

_____ (   )

∽ ∾ ∽ ∾

Today I am grateful for: _____

_____

_____

_____

_____

_____

_____

_____ (   )

My Kindnesses today: _____

_____

_____

_____

_____

_____

_____ (   )

People should ask themselves,
"Have you worked for something
larger than your own self interest?"
~ Jonathan Alter

September 12, _____

∽ ∽ ∽

Today I am grateful for: _____

_____

_____

_____

_____

_____ (   )

My Kindnesses today: _____

_____

_____

_____

_____

_____

_____ (   )

September 13, _____

~ ~ ~

Today I am grateful for: _____

_____

_____

_____

_____

_____

_____

_____ ( )

My Kindnesses today: _____

_____

_____

_____

_____

_____

_____ ( )

September 14, _____

～ ～ ～

Today I am grateful for: _____

_____

_____

_____

_____

_____

_____

_____ (   )

My Kindnesses today: _____

_____

_____

_____

_____

_____

_____ (   )

Appreciation can make a day - even change a life. Your willingness to put it into words is all that is necessary.

~ Margaret Cousins

∿ ∿ ∿

Today I am grateful for: _____

_____

_____

_____

_____

_____ (   )

My Kindnesses today: _____

_____

_____

_____

_____

_____ (   )

September 16, _____

∽ ∾ ∽

Today I am grateful for: _____

_____

_____

_____

_____

_____

_____

_____ (   )

My Kindnesses today: _____

_____

_____

_____

_____

_____

_____

_____ (   )

September 17, _____

∽ ∽ ∽

Today I am grateful for: _____

_____

_____

_____

_____

_____

_____ ( )

My Kindnesses today: _____

_____

_____

_____

_____

_____

_____ ( )

The greatest work that kindness does to others

is that it makes them kind themselves.

~ Amelia Earhart

September 18, _____

ᔕ ᔕ ᔕ

Today I am grateful for: _____

_____

_____

_____

_____

_____ ( )

My Kindnesses today: _____

_____

_____

_____

_____

_____ ( )

September 19, _____

～ ～ ～

Today I am grateful for: _____

_____

_____

_____

_____

_____

_____

_____ ( )

My Kindnesses today: _____

_____

_____

_____

_____

_____

_____

_____ ( )

September 20, _____

∾ ∾ ∾

Today I am grateful for: _____

_____

_____

_____

_____

_____

_____ (   )

My Kindnesses today: _____

_____

_____

_____

_____

_____

_____ (   )

Gratitude makes sense of our past,
brings peace for today
and creates a vision for tomorrow.

~ Melodie Beattie

ᔐ ᔐ ᔐ

Today I am grateful for: _____

_____

_____

_____

_____

_____ ( )

My Kindnesses today: _____

_____

_____

_____

_____ ( )

September 22, _____

∽ ∽ ∽

Today I am grateful for: _____

_____

_____

_____

_____

_____

_____ ( )

My Kindnesses today: _____

_____

_____

_____

_____

_____

_____ ( )

September 23, _____

∽ ∽ ∽

Today I am grateful for: _____

_____

_____

_____

_____

_____

_____ (   )

My Kindnesses today: _____

_____

_____

_____

_____

_____

_____ (   )

I awoke this morning with devout
thanksgiving for my friends,
the old and the new.

~ Ralph Waldo Emerson

September 24, _____

∽ ∽ ∽

Today I am grateful for: _____

_____

_____

_____

_____

_____ (   )

My Kindnesses today: _____

_____

_____

_____

_____

_____ (   )

∽ ∽ ∽

Today I am grateful for: _____

_____

_____

_____

_____

_____

_____

_____ (   )

My Kindnesses today: _____

_____

_____

_____

_____

_____

_____

_____ (   )

September 26, _____

∿ ∿ ∿

Today I am grateful for: _____

_____

_____

_____

_____

_____

_____

_____ (   )

My Kindnesses today: _____

_____

_____

_____

_____

_____ (   )

There is as much greatness of mind in acknowledging a good turn as in doing it.

~ Seneca

∾ ∾ ∾

Today I am grateful for: _____

_____

_____

_____

_____

_____

_____ (   )

My Kindnesses today: _____

_____

_____

_____

_____

_____

_____ (   )

September 28, _____

∾ ∾ ∾

Today I am grateful for: _____

_____

_____

_____

_____

_____

_____

_____ (   )

My Kindnesses today: _____

_____

_____

_____

_____

_____

_____ (   )

September 29, _____

∾ ∾ ∾

Today I am grateful for: _____

_____

_____

_____

_____

_____

_____ ( )

My Kindnesses today: _____

_____

_____

_____

_____

_____

_____ ( )

Our happiness and others' happiness

go together.

~ Matthieu Ricard

ᔆ ᔆ ᔆ

Today I am grateful for: _____

_____

_____

_____

_____

_____ (   )

My Kindnesses today: _____

_____

_____

_____

_____

_____ (   )

October 1, _____

∾ ∾ ∾

Today I am grateful for: _____

_____

_____

_____

_____

_____

_____ ( )

My Kindnesses today: _____

_____

_____

_____

_____

_____

_____ ( )

October 2, _____

∽ ∽ ∽ ∽

Today I am grateful for: _____

_____

_____

_____

_____

_____

_____ (   )

My Kindnesses today: _____

_____

_____

_____

_____

_____ (   )

Life without thankfulness is devoid of love and passion. Hope without thankfulness is lacking in fine perception. Faith without thankfulness lacks strength and fortitude. Every virtue divorced from thankfulness is maimed and limps along the spiritual road.

~ John Henry Jowett

Today I am grateful for: _____

_____

_____

_____

_____

_____ (   )

My Kindnesses today: _____

_____

_____

_____

_____

_____ (   )

October 4, _____

∾ ∾ ∾

Today I am grateful for: _____

_____

_____

_____

_____

_____

_____ (   )

My Kindnesses today: _____

_____

_____

_____

_____

_____

_____ (   )

October 5, _____

∾ ∾ ∾

Today I am grateful for: _____

_____

_____

_____

_____

_____

_____ ( )

My Kindnesses today: _____

_____

_____

_____

_____

_____

_____ ( )

Silent gratitude
isn't much use to anyone.

~ G.B. Stern

October 6, _____

ᔡ ᔡ ᔡ

Today I am grateful for: _____

_____

_____

_____

_____

_____

_____ (   )

My Kindnesses today: _____

_____

_____

_____

_____

_____ (   )

October 7, _____

～ ～ ～

Today I am grateful for: _____

_____

_____

_____

_____

_____

_____

_____ ( )

My Kindnesses today: _____

_____

_____

_____

_____

_____

_____

_____ ( )

October 8, _____

❧ ❧ ❧

Today I am grateful for: _____

_____

_____

_____

_____

_____

_____ ( )

My Kindnesses today: _____

_____

_____

_____

_____

_____

_____ ( )

Giving frees us from the familiar
territory of our own needs by opening
our mind to the unexplained worlds
occupied by the needs of others.

~ Barbara Bush

෬ ෬ ෬

Today I am grateful for: _____

_____

_____

_____

_____

_____ ( )

My Kindnesses today: _____

_____

_____

_____

_____

_____ ( )

❧ ❧ ❧

Today I am grateful for: _____

_____

_____

_____

_____

_____

_____

_____ ( )

My Kindnesses today: _____

_____

_____

_____

_____

_____

_____ ( )

October 11, _____

~ ~ ~

Today I am grateful for: _____

_____

_____

_____

_____

_____

_____(   )

My Kindnesses today: _____

_____

_____

_____

_____

_____

_____(   )

285

I think we should all ask ourselves,

"Am I doing something to

make the world a little better

for someone else?"

~ Elayne Bennett

October 12, _____

∾ ∾ ∾

Today I am grateful for: _____

_____

_____

_____

_____

_____ ( )

My Kindnesses today: _____

_____

_____

_____

_____

_____ ( )

October 13, _____

∽ ∽ ∽

Today I am grateful for: _____

_____

_____

_____

_____

_____

_____(   )

My Kindnesses today: _____

_____

_____

_____

_____

_____

_____(   )

October 14, _____

∽ ∽ ∽

Today I am grateful for: _____

_____

_____

_____

_____

_____

_____

_____ (   )

My Kindnesses today: _____

_____

_____

_____

_____

_____

_____ (   )

October 15, _____

If you want to turn your life around,
try thankfulness.
It will change your life mightily.
~ Gerald Good

∽ ∽ ∽

Today I am grateful for: _____

_____

_____

_____

_____

_____ (   )

My Kindnesses today: _____

_____

_____

_____

_____

_____ (   )

October 16, _____

∾ ∾ ∾

Today I am grateful for: _____

_____

_____

_____

_____

_____

_____ (   )

My Kindnesses today: _____

_____

_____

_____

_____

_____

_____ (   )

October 17, _____

∽ ∽ ∽

Today I am grateful for: _____

_____

_____

_____

_____

_____

_____

_____ (   )

My Kindnesses today: _____

_____

_____

_____

_____

_____

_____ (   )

The greatest use of life is to spend it
for something that will outlast it.

~ William James

∾ ∾ ∾

Today I am grateful for: _____

_____

_____

_____

_____

_____

_____ (   )

My Kindnesses today: _____

_____

_____

_____

_____

_____ (   )

October 19, _____

∽ ∽ ∽

Today I am grateful for: _____

_____

_____

_____

_____

_____

_____

_____ (   )

My Kindnesses today: _____

_____

_____

_____

_____

_____

_____

_____ (   )

October 20, _____

∾ ∾ ∾

Today I am grateful for: _____

_____

_____

_____

_____

_____

_____ ( )

My Kindnesses today: _____

_____

_____

_____

_____

_____

_____ ( )

I would maintain that thanks
are the highest form of thought;
and that gratitude is happiness
doubled by wonder.

~ G.K. Chesterton

∾ ∾ ∾

Today I am grateful for: _____

_____

_____

_____

_____

_____ (   )

My Kindnesses today: _____

_____

_____

_____

_____

_____

_____ (   )

295

October 22, _____

~ ~ ~

Today I am grateful for: _____

_____

_____

_____

_____

_____

_____ ( )

My Kindnesses today: _____

_____

_____

_____

_____

_____

_____ ( )

October 23, _____

∽ ∾ ∽

Today I am grateful for: _____

_____

_____

_____

_____

_____

_____

_____ (   )

My Kindnesses today: _____

_____

_____

_____

_____

_____

_____ (   )

When you are grateful, fear disappears
and abundance appears.

~ Anthony Robbins

October 24, _____

∾ ∾ ∾

Today I am grateful for: _____

_____

_____

_____

_____

_____

_____ (   )

My Kindnesses today: _____

_____

_____

_____

_____ (   )

October 25, _____

∽ ∽ ∽

Today I am grateful for: _____

_____

_____

_____

_____

_____

_____ (   )

My Kindnesses today: _____

_____

_____

_____

_____

_____

_____ (   )

October 26, _____

~ ~ ~

Today I am grateful for: _____

_____

_____

_____

_____

_____

_____ (   )

My Kindnesses today: _____

_____

_____

_____

_____

_____

_____ (   )

If a fellow isn't thankful for what
he's got, he isn't likely to be thankful
for what he's going to get.

~ Frank A. Clark

Today I am grateful for: _____

_____

_____

_____

_____

_____ ( )

My Kindnesses today: _____

_____

_____

_____

_____

_____ ( )

October 28, _____

∾ ∾ ∾

Today I am grateful for: _____

_____

_____

_____

_____

_____

_____ (   )

My Kindnesses today: _____

_____

_____

_____

_____

_____ (   )

October 29, _____

∽ ∾ ∽

Today I am grateful for: _____

_____

_____

_____

_____

_____

_____

_____ ( )

My Kindnesses today: _____

_____

_____

_____

_____

_____

_____ ( )

October 30, _____

Perhaps you will forget tomorrow
the kind words you say today,
but the recipient may cherish them
over a lifetime.

~ Dale Carnegie

❧ ❧ ❧

Today I am grateful for: _____

_____

_____

_____

_____

_____ (   )

My Kindnesses today: _____

_____

_____

_____

_____

_____

_____ (   )

304

October 31, _____

∾ ∾ ∾

Today I am grateful for: _____

_____

_____

_____

_____

_____

_____ (   )

My Kindnesses today: _____

_____

_____

_____

_____

_____ (   )

November 1, _____

∾ ∾ ∾

Today I am grateful for: _____

_____

_____

_____

_____

_____

_____

_____ (   )

My Kindnesses today: _____

_____

_____

_____

_____

_____

_____ (   )

If you want to better yourself,
better your fellow being.

~ Jaren L. Davis

November 2, _____

❧ ❧ ❧

Today I am grateful for: _____

_____

_____

_____

_____

_____

_____( )

My Kindnesses today: _____

_____

_____

_____

_____

_____

_____( )

307

November 3, _____

∾ ∾ ∾

Today I am grateful for: _____

_____

_____

_____

_____

_____

_____ ( )

My Kindnesses today: _____

_____

_____

_____

_____

_____

_____ ( )

In our daily lives, we must see that it is

not happiness that makes us grateful,

but the gratefulness that makes us happy.

~ Albert Clarke

෴ ෴ ෴

Today I am grateful for: _____

_____

_____

_____

_____

_____ (   )

My Kindnesses today: _____

_____

_____

_____

_____ (   )

November 5, _____

∽ ∾ ∽

Today I am grateful for: _____

_____

_____

_____

_____

_____

_____

_____ ( )

My Kindnesses today: _____

_____

_____

_____

_____

_____

_____ ( )

November 6, _____

∽ ∽ ∽

Today I am grateful for: _____

_____

_____

_____

_____

_____ (   )

My Kindnesses today: _____

_____

_____

_____

_____

_____ (   )

You have no cause for anything but gratitude and joy.

~ The Buddha

November 7, _____

∾ ∾ ∾

Today I am grateful for: _____

_____

_____

_____

_____

_____

_____ ( )

My Kindnesses today: _____

_____

_____

_____

_____

_____ ( )

November 8, _____

∾ ∾ ∾

Today I am grateful for: _____

_____

_____

_____

_____

_____

_____( )

My Kindnesses today: _____

_____

_____

_____

_____

_____

_____( )

November 9, _____

∽ ∾ ∽ ∾ ∽ ∾

Today I am grateful for: _____

_____

_____

_____

_____

_____

_____

_____ ( )

My Kindnesses today: _____

_____

_____

_____

_____

_____

_____ ( )

November 10, _____

*Those who bring sunshine to the lives of others
cannot keep it from themselves.*

~ James Matthew Barrie

❧ ❧ ❧

Today I am grateful for: _____

_____

_____

_____

_____

_____ (   )

My Kindnesses today: _____

_____

_____

_____

_____ (   )

᥍ ᥍ ᥍

Today I am grateful for: _____

_____

_____

_____

_____

_____

_____ ( )

My Kindnesses today: _____

_____

_____

_____

_____

_____ ( )

November 12, _____

∾ ∾ ∾

Today I am grateful for: _____

_____

_____

_____

_____

_____

_____ ( )

My Kindnesses today: _____

_____

_____

_____

_____

_____

_____ ( )

A person however learned and qualified in
his life's work, in whom gratitude is absent,
is devoid of that beauty of character
which makes personality fragrant.

~ Hazrat Inayat Khan

November 13, _____

∽ ∽ ∽ ∽

Today I am grateful for: _____

_____

_____

_____

_____

_____ (   )

My Kindnesses today: _____

_____

_____

_____

_____

_____ (   )

November 14, _____

∽ ∽ ∽ ∽

Today I am grateful for: _____

_____

_____

_____

_____

_____

_____

_____ ( )

My Kindnesses today: _____

_____

_____

_____

_____

_____

_____

_____ ( )

November 15, _____

~ ~ ~

Today I am grateful for: _____

_____

_____

_____

_____

_____

_____

_____ (   )

My Kindnesses today: _____

_____

_____

_____

_____

_____

_____ (   )

November 16, _____

Gratitude bestows reverence, allowing
us to encounter everyday epiphanies,
those transcendent moments of awe
that change forever how we experience
life and the world.

~ John Milton

∾ ∾ ∾

Today I am grateful for: _____

_____

_____

_____

_____

_____ (   )

My Kindnesses today: _____

_____

_____

_____

_____

_____ (   )

November 17, _____

∽ ∽ ∽

Today I am grateful for: _____

_____

_____

_____

_____

_____

_____ (   )

My Kindnesses today: _____

_____

_____

_____

_____

_____

_____ (   )

November 18, _____

∽ ∽ ∽

Today I am grateful for: _____

_____

_____

_____

_____

_____

_____ (   )

My Kindnesses today: _____

_____

_____

_____

_____

_____

_____ (   )

It's a sign of mediocrity when you demonstrate gratitude with moderation.

~ Roberto Benigni

November 19, _____

∽ ∽ ∽

Today I am grateful for: _____

_____

_____

_____

_____

_____

_____ (   )

My Kindnesses today: _____

_____

_____

_____

_____

_____

_____ (   )

November 20, _____

∾ ∾ ∾

Today I am grateful for: _____

_____

_____

_____

_____

_____

_____ (   )

My Kindnesses today: _____

_____

_____

_____

_____

_____

_____ (   )

∽ ∾ ∽ ∾

Today I am grateful for: _____

_____

_____

_____

_____

_____

_____ ( )

My Kindnesses today: _____

_____

_____

_____

_____

_____ ( )

November 22, _____

Three things in human life are important.
The first is to be kind. The second is
to be kind. The third is to be kind.

~ Henry James

ↄ ↄ ↄ

Today I am grateful for: _____

_____

_____

_____

_____ (   )

My Kindnesses today: _____

_____

_____

_____

_____

_____ (   )

327

November 23, _____

∽ ∽ ∽

Today I am grateful for: _____

_____

_____

_____

_____

_____

_____

_____ (   )

My Kindnesses today: _____

_____

_____

_____

_____

_____

_____ (   )

November 24, _____

❧ ❧ ❧

Today I am grateful for: _____

_____

_____

_____

_____

_____

_____

_____ (   )

My Kindnesses today: _____

_____

_____

_____

_____

_____

_____

_____ (   )

Joy is the simplest form of gratitude.

~ Karl Barth

November 25, _____

∽ ∽ ∽

Today I am grateful for: _____

_____

_____

_____

_____

_____

_____ (   )

My Kindnesses today: _____

_____

_____

_____

_____

_____ (   )

November 26, _____

∽ ∽ ∽

Today I am grateful for: _____

_____

_____

_____

_____

_____

_____

_____ (   )

My Kindnesses today: _____

_____

_____

_____

_____

_____

_____ (   )

November 27, _____

∾ ∾ ∾

Today I am grateful for: _____

_____

_____

_____

_____

_____

_____

_____ (   )

My Kindnesses today: _____

_____

_____

_____

_____

_____

_____ (   )

Open the door for other people.
Once you're there, you can go.

~ Michael Powell

November 28, _____

℘ ℘ ℘

Today I am grateful for: _____

_____

_____

_____

_____

_____ ( )

My Kindnesses today: _____

_____

_____

_____

_____

_____ ( )

November 29, _____

∾ ∾ ∾

Today I am grateful for: _____

_____

_____

_____

_____

_____

_____ ( )

My Kindnesses today: _____

_____

_____

_____

_____

_____

_____ ( )

November 30, _____

∾ ∾ ∾

Today I am grateful for: _____

_____

_____

_____

_____

_____

_____

_____ ( )

My Kindnesses today: _____

_____

_____

_____

_____

_____

_____ ( )

No one who achieves success does so without acknowledging the help of others. The wise and confident acknowledge this help with gratitude.

~ Alfred North Whitehead

∽ ∽ ∽

Today I am grateful for: _____

_____

_____

_____

_____

_____ (   )

My Kindnesses today: _____

_____

_____

_____

_____

_____ (   )

December 2, _____

∾ ∾ ∾

Today I am grateful for: _____

_____

_____

_____

_____

_____

_____ (   )

My Kindnesses today: _____

_____

_____

_____

_____

_____

_____ (   )

December 3, _____

∽ ∽ ∽

Today I am grateful for: _____

_____

_____

_____

_____

_____

_____ (   )

My Kindnesses today: _____

_____

_____

_____

_____

_____ (   )

The true meaning of life
is to plant trees under whose shade
you do not expect to sit.

~ Nelson Henderson

December 4, _____

∽ ∽ ∽

Today I am grateful for: _____

_____

_____

_____

_____

_____ ( )

My Kindnesses today: _____

_____

_____

_____

_____

_____

_____ ( )

December 5, _____

∽ ∽ ∽

Today I am grateful for: _____

_____

_____

_____

_____

_____

_____ (   )

My Kindnesses today: _____

_____

_____

_____

_____

_____

_____ (   )

∽ ∽ ∽

Today I am grateful for: _____

_____

_____

_____

_____

_____

_____

_____( )

My Kindnesses today: _____

_____

_____

_____

_____

_____

_____( )

He stands erect by bending over the fallen.

He rises by lifting others.

~ Robert G. Ingersoll

∽ ∽ ∽

Today I am grateful for: _____

_____

_____

_____

_____

_____

_____ ( )

My Kindnesses today: _____

_____

_____

_____

_____

_____

_____ ( )

December 8, _____

~ ~ ~

Today I am grateful for: _____

_____

_____

_____

_____

_____

_____

_____ (   )

My Kindnesses today: _____

_____

_____

_____

_____

_____

_____ (   )

December 9, _____

∽ ∽ ∽

Today I am grateful for: _____

_____

_____

_____

_____

_____

_____ ( )

My Kindnesses today: _____

_____

_____

_____

_____

_____ ( )

December 10, _____

There is something remarkable about

being grateful every morning.

~ Jay Hughes

∾ ∾ ∾

Today I am grateful for: _____

_____

_____

_____

_____

_____

_____ (   )

My Kindnesses today: _____

_____

_____

_____

_____

_____

_____ (   )

∽ ∽ ∽

Today I am grateful for: _____

_____

_____

_____

_____

_____

_____

_____ (   )

My Kindnesses today: _____

_____

_____

_____

_____

_____

_____ (   )

❧ ❧ ❧

Today I am grateful for: _____

_____

_____

_____

_____

_____

_____

_____ (   )

My Kindnesses today: _____

_____

_____

_____

_____

_____

_____

_____ (   )

Good things happen
when one does the right thing.
~ Michael Feinberg

December 13, _____

∾ ∾ ∾

Today I am grateful for: _____

_____

_____

_____

_____

_____ ( )

My Kindnesses today: _____

_____

_____

_____

_____

_____

_____ ( )

December 14, _____

～ ～ ～

Today I am grateful for: _____

_____

_____

_____

_____

_____

_____ (   )

My Kindnesses today: _____

_____

_____

_____

_____

_____

_____ (   )

∾ ∾ ∾

Today I am grateful for: _____

_____

_____

_____

_____

_____

_____ (   )

My Kindnesses today: _____

_____

_____

_____

_____

_____

_____ (   )

In ordinary life we hardly realize that
we receive a great deal more than we give,
and that it is only with gratitude
that life becomes rich.

~ Dietrich Bonhoeffer

Today I am grateful for: _____

_____

_____

_____

_____

_____ (   )

My Kindnesses today: _____

_____

_____

_____

_____

_____ (   )

December 17, _____

～ ～ ～

Today I am grateful for: _____

_____

_____

_____

_____

_____

_____ (   )

My Kindnesses today: _____

_____

_____

_____

_____

_____

_____ (   )

December 18, _____

∾ ∾ ∾

Today I am grateful for: _____

_____

_____

_____

_____

_____ ( )

My Kindnesses today: _____

_____

_____

_____

_____

_____ ( )

Deeds of kindness are equal in weight
to all the commandments.

~ Talmud

December 19, _____

∿ ∿ ∿

Today I am grateful for: _____

_____

_____

_____

_____

_____ (   )

My Kindnesses today: _____

_____

_____

_____

_____

_____

_____ (   )

December 20, _____

∽ ∽ ∽

Today I am grateful for: _____

_____

_____

_____

_____

_____

_____

_____ (   )

My Kindnesses today: _____

_____

_____

_____

_____

_____

_____

_____ (   )

∽ ∽ ∽

Today I am grateful for: _____

_____

_____

_____

_____

_____

_____ ( )

My Kindnesses today: _____

_____

_____

_____

_____

_____

_____ ( )

Treat everyone you meet as though they are the most important person you'll meet today.

~ Roger Dawson

December 22, _____

∽ ∽ ∽

Today I am grateful for: _____

_____

_____

_____

_____

_____ (   )

My Kindnesses today: _____

_____

_____

_____

_____

_____ (   )

December 23, _____

∽ ∽ ∽

Today I am grateful for: _____

_____

_____

_____

_____

_____

_____ (   )

My Kindnesses today: _____

_____

_____

_____

_____

_____ (   )

∾ ∾ ∾

Today I am grateful for: _____

_____

_____

_____

_____

_____

_____

_____ ( )

My Kindnesses today: _____

_____

_____

_____

_____

_____

_____ ( )

The best way to pay for a lovely

moment is to enjoy it.

~ Richard Bach

December 25, _____

            ∽ ∽ ∽

Today I am grateful for: _____

_____

_____

_____

_____

_____

_____ ( )

My Kindnesses today: _____

_____

_____

_____

_____

_____

_____ ( )

December 26, _____

❧ ❧ ❧

Today I am grateful for: _____

_____

_____

_____

_____

_____

_____ ( )

My Kindnesses today: _____

_____

_____

_____

_____

_____

_____ ( )

∾ ∾ ∾

Today I am grateful for: _____

_____

_____

_____

_____

_____

_____ (   )

My Kindnesses today: _____

_____

_____

_____

_____

_____

_____ (   )

*I'm grateful for the opportunity to
live on this beautiful and astonishing
planet Earth. In the morning,
I wake up with a sense of gratitude.*

~ Earl Nightingale

∾ ∾ ∾

Today I am grateful for: _____

_____

_____

_____

_____

_____ (   )

My Kindnesses today: _____

_____

_____

_____

_____

_____ (   )

December 29, _____

∾ ∾ ∾

Today I am grateful for: _____

_____

_____

_____

_____

_____

_____

_____ ( )

My Kindnesses today: _____

_____

_____

_____

_____

_____

_____

_____ ( )

December 30, _____

᪣ ᪣ ᪣

Today I am grateful for: _____

_____

_____

_____

_____

_____

_____

_____ (   )

My Kindnesses today: _____

_____

_____

_____

_____

_____

_____ (   )

365

December 31, _____

Ask yourself whether on your deathbed you will believe you have lived a good life - taking advantage of your gifts, striving to be excellent at what you do, and to do that in the service of others. Are you living life to the fullest, and if not, why not?

~ Peter Reiling

❧ ❧ ❧

Today I am grateful for: _____

_____

_____

_____

_____

_____ (   )

My Kindnesses today: _____

_____

_____

_____

_____ (   )

Carryover pages

_____

_____

_____

_____

_____

_____

_____

_____

_____

_____

_____

_____

Go into the world and do well.
But more importantly,
go into the world and do good.

~ Minor Myers Jr.

My Year of Kindness

date _____ year _____

_____
_____
_____
_____
_____
_____
_____
_____
_____
_____
_____
_____
_____
_____
_____
_____
_____
_____
_____

Endnotes

❦ ❦ ❦

[1] Csikszentmihalyi, M. 1999. If We Are So Rich, Why Aren't We Happy? *American Psychologist. Volume 54(10) October 1999* p 821-827.

[2] Fowler, J., and Christakis, N. 2010. Cooperative behavior cascades in human social networks. *Proceedings of the National Academy of Sciences vol. 107 no.12 March 23, 2010.*

[3] Van Praag, B., and Frijters, P. 1999. The Measurement of Welfare and Well-Being. *Well-Being: The Foundations of Hedonic Psychology.* eds Kahneman, D., Diener, E. & Schwartz, N. New York: Russell Sage.

[4] Ryan, R. M., and Deci, E. L. 2001. On Happiness and Human Potentials: A Review of Research on Hedonic and Eudaimonic Well-Being. *Annual Review of Psychology. 52:141-66.*

[5] Kennedy, R. Campaign speech March 18, 1968.

[6] Field, T., Hernandez-Reif, M., Quintino, O., Schanberg, S., and Kuhn, C. 1998. Elder Retired Volunteers Benefit from Giving Massage Therapy to Infants. *Journal of Applied Gerontology* 17: 229-239.

[7] Luks, A., and Payne, P. 1991. *The Healing Power of Doing Good: The Health and Spiritual Benefits of Helping Others.* New York: Fawcett Columbine.

[8] Brooks, A. *Gross National Happiness.* 2008. New York: Basic Books. (Citing Davis, J., Smith, T., Marsden, P. (principal investigators) *General Social Surveys.* 1972-2004.); Kloseck, M., Crilly, R. G., Mannell, R. 2006. Involving the community elderly in the planning and provision of health services: Predictors of volunteerism and leadership. *Canadian Journal on Aging* 25 (1): 77 - 91 (2006) 77; Borgonovi, F. 2008. Doing well by doing good. The relationship between formal volunteering and self-reported health and happiness. *Journal of Social Science and Medicine 66, 2321- 2334.*

[9] Brooks, A. 2006. *Who Really Cares?* Cambridge, MA: Basic Books.

[10] Schwartz, C. et al., 2003. Altruistic Social Interest Behaviors Are Associated with Better Mental Health. *Psychosomatic Medicine 65 (2003):* 778-785; Goldberg, C., "For Good Health it is Better to Give, Science Suggests," *Boston Globe*, November 28, 2003; Pearsall, P. 1996. *The Pleasure Prescription: To Love, to Work, to Play – Life in the Balance.* Alameda, CA: Hunter House; Luks, A. & Payne, P. 1991. *The Healing Power of Doing Good: The Health and Spiritual Benefits of Helping Others.* New York: Fawcett Columbine.

[11] Brooks, A. 2006. *Who Really Cares?* Cambridge, MA: Basic Books.

[12] Brooks, A. 2006. *Who Really Cares?* Cambridge, MA: Basic Books.

[13] Christakis, N. & Fowler, J. 2009. *Connected: The Surprising Power of Our Social Networks and How They Shape Our Lives.* New York: Little Brown; Fowler, J. & Christakis, N. 2010. Cooperative behavior cascades in human social networks. *Proceedings of the National Academy of Sciences vol. 107 no.12 March 23, 2010.* (A $10,000 increase in income is associate with a 2% increased chance of being happy, while a person is about 10% more likely to be happy if his friend has a happy friend, and about 6% more likely to be happy if his friend has a friend who has a happy friend.)

[14] B Emmons, RD., & McCullough, M. 2003. Counting blessings versus burdens: An

experimental investigation of gratitude and subjective well-being in daily life. *Journal of Personality and Social Psychology,* Vol. 84, No. 2: 377–389; Otake, K., Shimai, S., Tanaka-Matsumi, T., Otsui, K, & Fredrickson, B. 2006. Happy People Become Happier Through Kindness: A counting kindness intervention. *Journal of Happiness Studies 7:361–375.*

[15] Beermann, U., Park, N., Peterson, C., Ruch, W., & Seligman, M.E.P. 2007. Strengths of Character, Orientations to Happiness and Life Satisfaction. *The Journal of Positive Psychology, 2(3): 149-156 July 2007.*

About the Author

❧ ❧ ❧

Psychologist Pamela Paresky received her PhD in Human Development and Psychology from the University of Chicago. Her research at the National Opinion Research Center (NORC) focused on happiness and *Flow*, the expression of Dr. Csikszentmihalyi's theory of optimal experience.

Before her work at NORC, Dr. Paresky conducted field research in the North West Territories of Canada where she lived with and photographed the Inuit; and in New York City where she studied the city's Native American population. She later consulted for Castle Rock Entertainment as a technical advisor in psychology, taught college courses in cultural anthropology, and practiced psychotherapy with a specialization in marriage, family, and children. Dr. Paresky's work has been published in several periodicals including *The Washington Post, Aspen Philanthropist, and Aspen Peak Magazine* among others, as well as online at *AspenPost.net* and *BackboneAmerica.net*.

Dr. Paresky consults for nonprofits and serves on the National Advisory Board of the Miami-based *United Way Center for Excellence in Early Education* as well as the Society of Fellows Advisory Committee at *The Aspen Institute*, the Alumni Council for *Phillips Academy* (Andover), The Human Development Steering Committee of the *Statue of Responsibility Foundation*, and the Advisory Board of *Child Help River Bridge*, a Child Advocacy center. In addition to her interdisciplinary PhD, Dr. Paresky holds a Master's degree in Clinical Psychology and a Bachelor's degree in Anthropology.

Her current research focuses on helping people lead meaningful lives.

❧ ❧ ❧

56540266R00228

Made in the USA
San Bernardino, CA
12 November 2017